Classic

IRISH

Classic
IRISH

A selection of the best traditional Irish food

MATTHEW DRENNAN

HERMES
HOUSE

For Kevin, Audrey, Liam, Jimmy, Aileen, Jim, Betty and Mark with love.

This edition published in 1999 by Hermes House

Hermes House is an imprint of
Anness Publishing Limited
88-89 Blackfriars Road
London SE1 8HA

ISBN 1 84038 004 7

Publisher Joanna Lorenz
Senior Cookery Editor Linda Fraser
Cookery Editor Maggie Mayhew
Designer Annie Moss
Illustrator Madeleine David
Photographer Thomas Odulate
Food for photography Janet Smith, assisted by Lucy McKelvie
Stylist Marion Price
Special photography Kevin Drennan

Printed and bound in Singapore

3 5 7 9 10 8 6 4 2

For all recipes, quantities are given in both metric and imperial measures and, where appropriate,
measures are also given in standard cups and spoons. Follow one set, but not a mixture,
because they are not interchangeable.

CONTENTS

FOREWORD

As an Irishman I'm biased towards the traditional dishes and recipes of Ireland. But it's my love of everything simple and natural in the kitchen that truly draws me to this unassuming style of cooking.

In the past and perhaps in less progressive times, the national food of this country was far from "gourmet" and cooking existed to feed the appetite, not the tastebuds. However, there has been something of a renaissance in Irish cooking and today cooks all over the country are resurrecting some of the classic dishes created by this small and unassuming island.

It will become quickly apparent when cooking Irish-style, that no great culinary skills or techniques are required. This book highlights the premium products that Ireland produces – from the farmers and fishermen to the market gardeners and cheese-makers who have one common bond, their commitment to excellence.

Like the recipes themselves, the ingredients are simple and easily obtained. The key is to choose the best and the freshest – as the Irish would say, "sure, you're half way there!"

For most of the recipes you'll find the extraordinary or exotic are few and far between; on the whole a trip to the local market will cover everything you need. Irish cooks have always been heavy handed with their use of dairy produce, so I've modified some of the recipes in line with today's healthier style of living, although you'll find the odd "gallon" of cream used here and there in those recipes which would be considered too sacrilegious to interfere with, but as they say, "a little of what you fancy does you good!"

Sláinte! (that's Irish for "cheers!").

MATTHEW DRENNAN

INTRODUCTION

If you have the pleasure of visiting any restaurant in Ireland today, you will be warmly greeted with a wealth of the world's cuisines. However, from Antrim in the north to the southern most tip of County Kerry, you'll find, at the heart of every kitchen, a simple, honest, local approach that is – classic Irish cookery.

Of course, many of Ireland's fine dishes such as Irish Stew or Colcannon were born out of necessity in poorer times, but there are two factors that have always made these simple recipes great: the land and the sea. The rich fertile soil and lush meadows nurture the finest beef, dairy products and vegetables in the world, while the miles of coastline are rich in all kinds of fish.

In a small country like Ireland, news travels fast and if a recipe is a success in one region it soon becomes a national favourite. Mysteriously though, even with something as well known as Coddle, from house to house, farm to farm or pub to pub, no two recipes are ever quite the same.

One thing that remains constant, wherever you go, is the potato. It is to the Irish people

Clonakility Blackpudding Company in County Cork (left), the rugged beauty of Brandon Creek on the Dingle Peninsula (above) and the tranquility of Lough Corrib in County Mayo (right) are but a few of the simple, natural attractions of Irish living.

what pasta is to the Italians. In fact, Ireland's bleakest period of history was in 1845–46 when the national crop failed, thus causing the great famine. Nowadays, there are no worries about that, but this versatile vegetable forms the backbone of many meals. As you will discover, it makes an appearance not just in savoury dishes, but in Irish cakes and desserts, too.

Potatoes fall into two main categories: waxy and floury. For most recipes in this book the floury varieties, such as Pentland Crown, King Edward or Maris Piper are preferable as they mash better. Take care to peel away the minimum of skin as all the nutrients lie just beneath the surface.

They say that the only possible way to walk down any street in Ireland without passing a pub is to go in to each one! So, not surprisingly, you will find that a few recipes feature one or two well known drinks such as Guinness from Dublin, Murphy's from Cork and whiskey from just about anywhere.

Apart from soups, which are traditionally eaten with stacks of freshly baked soda bread at lunchtime, there are very few starters featured in this cookery book, but you could do a lot worse than enjoy a plate of fresh oysters or some thin slices of smoked salmon embellished with little more than a wedge of lemon.

Breadmaking and baking are still a very important part of Irish life, particularly in the rural areas where the day starts with

soda bread and griddle cakes and ends in the evening with a chunk of Porter Cake and a small glass of whiskey, just to help you sleep well, of course!

Irish food is simply prepared and served without fuss or ceremony. Family and good friends may come first, but good food and plenty of drink will always play host to every occasion.

LEEK AND THYME SOUP

A filling, heart-warming soup which can be liquidised to a smooth purée or served as it is here, in its original peasant style.

INGREDIENTS
900g/2lb leeks
450g/1lb potatoes
115g/4oz/8 tbsp butter
2 large thyme sprigs
300ml/½ pint/1¼ cups
semi-skimmed milk
salt and ground black pepper
60ml/4 tbsp double cream,
to serve
thyme, to garnish (optional)

SERVES 4

1 Top and tail the leeks. If you are using big winter leeks strip away all the coarser outer leaves, then cut the leeks into thick slices. Wash under cold running water.

2 Cut the potatoes into rough dice, about 2.5cm/1in, and dry on kitchen paper.

3 Melt the butter in a large saucepan and add the leeks and 1 thyme sprig. Cover and cook for 4–5 minutes until softened. Add the potato pieces and just enough cold water to cover the vegetables. Re-cover and cook over a low heat for 30 minutes.

4 Pour in the semi-skimmed milk and the seasoning, cover and simmer for a further 30 minutes. You will find that some of the potato breaks up leaving you with a semi-purée and rather lumpy soup.

5 Remove the thyme sprig (the leaves will have fallen into the soup) and serve, adding a tablespoon of cream and a garnish of thyme to each portion, if using.

YELLOW BROTH

This is one of many versions of this famous Northern Irish soup which is both thickened with and given its flavour by oatmeal.

INGREDIENTS

25g/1oz/2 tbsp butter
1 onion, finely chopped
1 celery stick, finely chopped
1 carrot, finely chopped
25g/1oz/2 tbsp plain flour
900ml/1½ pints/3¾ cups chicken stock
25g/1oz/2 tbsp medium oatmeal
115g/4oz spinach, chopped
30ml/2 tbsp cream
salt and ground black pepper
fresh parsley, to garnish (optional)

SERVES 4

1 Melt the butter in a large saucepan. Add the onion, celery and carrot and cook for about 2 minutes until the onion is soft.

2 Stir in the flour and cook gently for a further 1 minute, stirring constantly. Pour in the chicken stock, bring to the boil and cover. Reduce the heat and simmer for 30 minutes, until the vegetables are tender.

3 Stir in the oatmeal and chopped spinach and then cook for a further 15 minutes, stirring occasionally.

4 Stir in the cream and season well. Serve, garnished with parsley, if using.

CELERY SOUP

Mild celery with a hint of nutmeg – this classic creamy soup makes a perfect starter.

INGREDIENTS
1 small head of celery
1 onion, finely chopped
1 small garlic clove, crushed
few parsley sprigs, chopped
2 bay leaves
1 thyme sprig
600ml/1 pint/2½ cups semi-skimmed milk
25g/1oz/2 tbsp butter, softened
25g/1oz/2 tbsp plain flour
pinch of grated nutmeg
1 egg yolk, beaten
salt and ground black pepper
chopped fresh parsley, to garnish
croûtons, to serve

SERVES 4

COOK'S TIP
If you do not have a blender or food processor, pass the soup through a metal sieve, pressing the cooked vegetables through with the back of a spoon.

1 Break the head of celery into stalks and wash thoroughly. Trim the root ends. Chop the stalks and leaves and put them into a large saucepan.

2 Add the chopped onion, garlic, parsley, bay leaves, thyme and just enough water to cover. Bring to the boil and simmer the vegetables, uncovered, over a gentle heat for about 35 minutes.

3 In a clean saucepan, bring the semi-skimmed milk to the boil. Knead the butter and flour together to make a roux and whisk into the hot milk until just thickened. Cook over a gentle heat for about 10 minutes, stirring occasionally. Pour into the celery mixture and cook for 5 minutes.

4 Remove the bay leaves and thyme. Using a ladle, spoon the soup into a blender or food processor and process for 1 minute until smooth. Return to a clean saucepan and season well.

5 Stir in the nutmeg and beaten egg yolk. Bring almost to boiling point, then serve garnished with parsley leaves and croûtons.

PEA AND HAM SOUP

The main ingredient for this dish is bacon hock which is the narrow piece of bone cut from a leg of ham. You could use a piece of belly of pork instead, if you like, and remove it before serving with the finished soup.

INGREDIENTS
450g/1lb/2½ cups green split peas
4 rindless streaky bacon rashers
1 onion, roughly chopped
2 carrots, sliced
1 celery stick, sliced
2.4 litres/4 pints/10 cups cold water
1 thyme sprig
2 bay leaves
1 large potato, roughly diced
1 bacon hock
ground black pepper

SERVES 4

1 Put the peas into a bowl, cover with cold water and leave to soak overnight.

2 Cut the streaky bacon into small pieces. In a large saucepan, dry-fry the bacon for 4–5 minutes or until crisp. Remove from the pan with a slotted spoon.

3 Add the chopped onion, carrots and celery stick to the fat in the pan and cook for 3–4 minutes until the onion is softened, but not brown. Return the bacon to the pan with the water.

4 Drain the split peas and add to the pan with the thyme, bay leaves, potato and bacon hock. Bring to the boil, reduce the heat, cover and cook gently for 1 hour.

5 Remove the thyme, bay leaves and hock. Process the soup in a blender or food processor until smooth. Return to a clean pan. Cut the meat from the hock and add to the soup. Season with lots of black pepper.

NETTLE SOUP

A country-style soup which is a tasty variation of the classic Irish potato soup. Use wild nettles if you can find them, or a washed head of round lettuce if you prefer.

INGREDIENTS
115g/4oz/8 tbsp butter
450g/1lb large onions, sliced
450g/1lb potatoes, cut into chunks
750ml/1¼ pints/3 cups chicken stock
25g/1oz nettle leaves
small bunch of chives, snipped
salt and ground black pepper
double cream, to serve

SERVES 4

1 Melt the butter in a large saucepan and add the sliced onions. Cover and cook for 5 minutes until just softened. Add the potatoes to the saucepan with the chicken stock. Cover and cook for 25 minutes.

2 Wearing rubber gloves, remove the nettle leaves from their stalks. Wash the leaves under cold running water, then dry on kitchen paper. Add to the saucepan and cook for a further 5 minutes.

3 Ladle the soup into a blender or food processor and process until smooth. Return to a clean saucepan and season well. Stir in the chives and serve with a swirl of cream and a sprinkling of pepper.

ROAST CHICKEN WITH HERB AND ORANGE BREAD STUFFING

 ender roast chicken scented with orange and herbs, served with a light gravy.

INGREDIENTS
2 onions
25g/1oz/2 tbsp butter
150g/5oz/2½ cups soft white breadcrumbs
30ml/2 tbsp chopped fresh mixed herbs
grated rind of 1 orange
1.5kg/3½lb chicken with giblets
1 carrot, sliced
1 bay leaf
1 thyme sprig
900ml/1½ pints/3¾ cups cold water
15ml/1 tbsp tomato purée
10ml/2 tsp cornflour, mixed with
15ml/1 tablespoon cold water
salt and ground black pepper
chopped fresh thyme, to garnish

SERVES 4–6

1 Preheat the oven to 200°C/400°F/Gas 6. Finely chop 1 onion. Melt the butter in a pan and add the onion. Cook for 3–4 minutes until soft. Stir in the breadcrumbs, fresh herbs and orange rind. Season well.

2 Remove the giblets from the chicken and put aside. Wash the cavity of the chicken and dry well with kitchen paper. Spoon in the herb and orange stuffing, then rub a little butter into the breast and season it well. Put the chicken into a roasting tin and cook in the oven for 20 minutes, then reduce the heat to 180°C/350°F/Gas 4 and cook for a further 1 hour.

3 Put the giblets, the other onion, the carrot, bay leaf, thyme and cold water into a large pan. Bring to the boil, then simmer while the chicken is roasting.

4 Remove the chicken from the tin. Skim off the fat from the cooking juices, strain the juices and stock into a pan and discard the giblets and vegetables. Simmer for about 5 more minutes. Whisk in the tomato purée.

5 Whisk the cornflower paste into the gravy and cook for 1 minute. Season well and serve with the chicken, garnished with thyme.

CHICKEN, LEEK AND BACON CASSEROLE

 moist whole chicken, braised on a bed of leeks and bacon and topped with a creamy tarragon sauce.

INGREDIENTS
15ml/1 tbsp vegetable oil
25g/1oz/2 tbsp butter
1.5kg/3½lb chicken
225g/8oz streaky bacon
450g/1lb leeks
250ml/8fl oz/1 cup chicken stock
250ml/8fl oz/1 cup double cream
15ml/1 tbsp chopped fresh tarragon
salt and ground black pepper

SERVES 4–6

1 Preheat the oven to 180°C/350°F/Gas 4. Heat the oil and melt the butter in a large flameproof casserole. Add the chicken and cook it breast side down for 5 minutes until golden. Remove from the casserole.

2 Dice the bacon and add to the casserole. Cook for 4–5 minutes until golden.

3 Top and tail the leeks, cut them into 2.5cm/1in pieces and add to the bacon. Cook for 5 minutes until the leeks begin to brown. Put the chicken on top of the bacon and leeks. Cover and put into the oven. Cook for 1½ hours.

4 Remove the chicken, bacon and leeks from the casserole. Skim the fat from the juices. Pour in the stock and the cream and bring to the boil. Cook for 4–5 minutes until slightly reduced and thickened.

5 Stir in the tarragon and seasoning (it may only need pepper). Serve chicken slices with the bacon, leeks and a little sauce.

CODDLE

Stroll round Dublin on a Saturday night and you will find numerous variations of this traditional favourite dish. The basic ingredients, however, are the same wherever you go – potatoes, sausages and bacon.

INGREDIENTS
4 back bacon rashers
15ml/1 tbsp vegetable oil
2 large onions, chopped
2 garlic cloves, crushed
8 large pork sausages
4 large potatoes
1.5ml/¼ tsp dried sage
300ml/½ pint/1¼ cups chicken stock
30ml/2 tbsp chopped fresh parsley
salt and ground black pepper
soda bread, to serve

SERVES 4

1 Preheat the oven to 180°C/350°F/Gas 4. Cut the bacon into 2.5cm/1in strips.

2 Heat the oil in a frying pan and fry the bacon for 2 minutes. Add the onions and cook for a further 5–6 minutes until golden. Add the garlic and cook for 1 minute, then remove from the pan and set aside.

3 Add the pork sausages to the frying pan and cook on all sides for 5–6 minutes until golden brown.

4 Slice the potatoes thinly and arrange in the base of a large, buttered ovenproof dish. Spoon the bacon and onion mixture on top. Season with the ground black pepper and sprinkle with the sage.

5 Pour over the chicken stock and top with the sausages. Cover and cook in the oven for 1 hour. Serve with fresh soda bread.

BOILED HAM AND CABBAGE

no-nonsense dish that is full of warming winter flavours and very easy to make.

INGREDIENTS
1.25kg/3lb ham, in one piece
2 bay leaves
12 peppercorns
1 celery stick
1–2 onions, halved
2 large carrots
1 large Savoy cabbage
salt and ground black pepper
chopped fresh parsley, to garnish
boiled potatoes, to serve (optional)

SERVES 6

1 Drain the water from the ham if you have soaked it. Weigh the meat to calculate the cooking time. Put the ham into a large saucepan and cover with cold water.

2 Add the bay leaves, peppercorns, celery stick, onions and carrots. Bring to the boil, reduce the heat, cover and simmer for 25 minutes per 450g/1lb plus 25 minutes.

3 Carefully lift out the ham and set it aside. Drain the cooking liquid into a clean saucepan and bring to the boil.

4 Meanwhile, discard the outer leaves of the cabbage. Tear the remaining leaves, including the heart, into pieces, discarding any of the tough stalks. Add to the cooking liquid and cook, uncovered, for 20 minutes until tender. Taste for seasoning – you may not have to add any.

5 Serve slices of the warm ham on a bed of cabbage with a little of the cooking liquid poured over the top. Garnish with the chopped parsley and serve with boiled potatoes, if liked.

COOK'S TIP
It is always difficult to tell how salty a piece of ham is going to be unless you buy it from a regular source. If in doubt, soak it in cold water for several hours or overnight, changing the water at least once.

RABBIT
STEW

This is a hearty winter stew which includes the classic combination of rabbit and butter beans, delicately flavoured with garlic and bacon.

INGREDIENTS
115g/4oz/¾ cup butter beans
1.25kg/3lb rabbit, jointed
25g/1oz/2 tbsp plain flour
25g/1oz/2 tbsp lard
2 streaky bacon rashers, finely chopped
1 onion, chopped
1 garlic clove, crushed
15ml/1 tbsp tomato purée
450g/1lb carrots, sliced
1 celery stick, sliced
2 bay leaves
600ml/1 pint/2½ cups chicken stock
salt and ground black pepper
mashed potato, to serve (optional)

SERVES 4

1 Put the butter beans into a bowl, cover with cold water and leave to soak thoroughly overnight.

2 Preheat the oven to 180°C/350°F/Gas 4. Put the rabbit joints, flour and seasoning into a bag and shake until the rabbit pieces are well and evenly coated.

3 Melt the lard in a flameproof casserole. Fry the rabbit over a medium heat until golden. Remove from the dish and set aside. Add the bacon, onion and garlic and cook for 4–5 minutes until the onion is just soft.

4 Stir in the tomato purée and cook for 1 minute. Return the rabbit to the dish with the carrot, celery and bay leaves. Pour in the stock, cover and cook for 1 hour.

5 Remove from the oven. Drain the butter beans and stir them into the casserole. Replace the lid and return to the oven for a further 50 minutes. Check the seasoning and serve with mashed potato, if liked.

IRISH STEW

S imple and delicious, this is the quintessential Irish main course. Traditionally, mutton chops are used, but as they are harder to find these days you can use lamb instead.

INGREDIENTS

1.25kg/3lb boneless lamb chops
15ml/1 tbsp vegetable oil
3 large onions
4 large carrots
900ml/1½ pints/3¾ cups water
4 large potatoes, cut into chunks
1 large thyme sprig
15g/½oz/1 tbsp butter
15ml/1 tbsp chopped fresh parsley
salt and ground black pepper
Savoy cabbage, to serve (optional)

SERVES 4

1 Trim any fat from the lamb. Heat the oil in a flameproof casserole and brown the meat on both sides. Remove from the pan.

2 Cut the onions into quarters and thickly slice the carrots. Add to the casserole and cook for 5 minutes until the onions are browned. Return the meat to the pan with the water. Bring to the boil, reduce the heat, cover and simmer for 1 hour.

3 Add the potatoes to the pan with the thyme and cook for a further 1 hour.

4 Leave the stew to settle for a few minutes. Remove the fat from the liquid with a ladle, then pour off the liquid into a clean saucepan. Stir in the butter and the parsley. Season well and pour back into the casserole. Serve with Savoy cabbage, if liked.

SPICED BEEF

Christmas in Ireland would not be complete without a cold side of spiced beef to see you through the holiday season. Make sure you allow plenty of time (at least ten days) for the meat to absorb the spices and marinade, as this is what makes it so tender and full of flavour.

INGREDIENTS
225g/8oz/1 cup sea salt
1.25kg/2½lb silverside of beef or brisket, boned and untied
50g/2oz/4 tbsp brown sugar
2.5ml/½ tsp ground allspice
2.5ml/½ tsp ground cloves
2.5ml/½ tsp grated nutmeg
1 bay leaf, crushed
15ml/1 tbsp saltpetre
50g/2oz/1 tbsp black treacle
2 carrots, sliced
1 onion, quartered
ground black pepper
pickles and bread, to serve (optional)

SERVES 8

1 Rub the salt into the beef and leave in a cool place overnight.

2 In a bowl, mix the brown sugar, allspice, cloves, nutmeg, bay leaf, saltpetre and ground black pepper. Remove the beef from the salt and juices and wipe dry with kitchen paper. Sprinkle with the spice mixture and leave in a cool place overnight.

3 Lightly warm the black treacle and pour it over the meat. Leave to marinate for 1 week, turning once a day.

4 Roll up the beef and secure it with string. Put it into a large pan of boiling water with the carrots and onion. Bring to the boil, lower the heat, cover and simmer for 3 hours. Leave to cool in the liquid.

5 Transfer the beef to a board or a large plate. Balance another board on top, weight it down and leave for at least 8 hours. Carve and serve the meat cold with pickles and bread, if liked.

STEAK WITH STOUT AND POTATOES

This recipe uses the finest and most famous of all the Emerald Isle's ingredients: Irish beef, Murphy's stout from Cork and, of course, potatoes. You can use any stout, but Murphy's is less bitter than most.

INGREDIENTS

675g/1½lb stewing or braising steak
15ml/1 tbsp vegetable oil
25g/1oz/2 tbsp butter
225g/8oz baby or pickling onions
175ml/6fl oz/¾ cup stout
300ml/½ pint/1¼ cups beef stock
bouquet garni
675g/1½lb potatoes, cut into thick slices
225g/8oz field mushrooms, sliced if large
15g/½oz/1 tbsp plain flour
2.5ml/½ tsp mild mustard
salt and ground black pepper
chopped thyme sprigs, to garnish

SERVES 4

1 Trim any excess fat from the steak and cut into four pieces. Season both sides of the meat. Heat the oil and half the butter in a large heavy pan. Brown the meat on both sides, taking care not to burn the butter. Remove from the pan and set aside.

2 Add the baby onions to the pan and brown for 3–4 minutes. Return the steak to the pan. Pour over the stout and stock and season to taste.

3 Add the bouquet garni and top with the potato slices. Cover with a tight-fitting lid and simmer over a gentle heat for 1 hour.

4 Add the mushrooms. Replace the lid and cook for a further 30 minutes. Remove the meat and vegetables with a slotted spoon and arrange on a platter.

5 Mix the remaining butter with the flour to make a roux. Whisk a little at a time into the cooking liquid. Stir in the mustard. Cook for 2–3 minutes until thickened. Season and pour over the meat. Garnish with plenty of thyme sprigs.

COOK'S TIP
Put the onions in a bowl and cover with boiling water. Leave to soak for about 5 minutes and drain. The skins should peel away easily.

GUINNESS AND OYSTER PIE

L ayers of crisp puff pastry encase a tasty rich stew of tender beef and fresh oysters.

INGREDIENTS

450g/1lb stewing or braising steak
25g/1oz/2 tbsp plain flour
15ml/1 tbsp vegetable oil
25g/1oz/2 tbsp butter
1 onion, sliced
150ml/¼ pint/⅔ cup Guinness
150ml/¼ pint/⅔ cup beef stock
5ml/1 tsp sugar
bouquet garni
12 oysters, opened
350g/12oz puff pastry
1 egg, beaten
salt and ground black pepper
chopped fresh parsley, to garnish

SERVES 4

1 Preheat the oven to 180°C/350°F/Gas 4. Trim any excess fat from the meat and cut into 2.5cm/1in dice. Place in a bag with the flour and plenty of seasoning. Shake until the meat is well coated.

2 Heat the oil and butter in a flameproof casserole and fry the meat for 10 minutes until well sealed and browned all over. Add the onion and continue cooking for 2–3 minutes until just softened.

3 Pour in the Guinness and stock. Add the sugar and bouquet garni. Cover and cook in the oven for 1¼ hours.

4 Remove from the oven, spoon into a pie dish (about 1.2 litres/2 pints/5 cups) and leave to cool for 15 minutes. Increase the oven temperature to 200°C/400°F/Gas 6.

5 Meanwhile, remove the oysters from their shells and wash. Dry on kitchen paper and stir into the steak and Guinness.

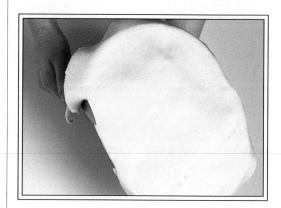

6 Roll out the pastry large enough to fit the pie dish. Brush the edge of the dish with beaten egg and lay the pastry over the top. Trim neatly and decorate. Brush with the remaining egg and cook for 25 minutes until puffed and golden. Serve immediately, garnished with parsley.

PRAWNS WITH GARLIC BREADCRUMBS

Fresh Dublin Bay prawns, also known by their French name, *langoustine*, are a delight to eat, especially when smothered in garlic butter and topped with fresh golden breadcrumbs. Halve this recipe for starter portions.

INGREDIENTS

32 Dublin Bay prawns
350g/12oz/1½ cups butter, softened
8 garlic cloves, chopped
30ml/2 tbsp chopped fresh parsley
4 spring onions, finely chopped
15ml/1 tbsp wholegrain mustard
115g/4oz/2 cups fresh white breadcrumbs
ground black pepper
fresh parsley, to garnish
brown bread, to serve

SERVES 4

1 Bring a large pan of water to the boil. Drop in the prawns. Cook until they float on top of the water. Drain and refresh under cold water, then shell.

2 Preheat the oven to 200°C/400°F/Gas 6. Place the butter, garlic, parsley, spring onions, mustard and plenty of ground black pepper in a bowl. Beat until well blended.

3 Share the prawns among four individual ovenproof dishes. Divide the butter among them and spread it over the prawns with the back of a knife. Sprinkle with the fresh breadcrumbs.

4 Place the dishes in the oven and cook for about 15 minutes, or until the breadcrumbs are golden brown. Garnish the dishes with fresh parsley and serve with brown bread.

DRESSED CRAB

D ressed crab has topped the menu in Irish restaurants for many years. It is traditionally served in the crab shell, but you could use individual ovenproof dishes if you prefer.

INGREDIENTS
150ml/¼ pint/⅔ cup milk
40g/1½oz/3 tbsp butter
15ml/1 tbsp plain flour
350g/12oz fresh white crab meat
5ml/1 tsp French mustard
275g/10oz/5 cups fresh breadcrumbs
30ml/2 tbsp snipped fresh chives
salt and ground black pepper
snipped chives and chopped parsley,
to garnish

SERVES 4

1 Preheat the oven to 200°C/400°F/Gas 6. Bring the milk to the boil. In another saucepan, melt 15g/½oz/1 tbsp of the butter. Stir in the flour and cook for 1 minute. Gradually whisk in the milk, a little at a time, until smooth and thick. Cook over a gentle heat for 5 minutes. Allow to cool.

2 Put the crab meat into a bowl with the mustard, 150g/5oz/2½ cups of the breadcrumbs and the snipped chives. Season with salt and ground black pepper. Stir into the white sauce and mix well.

3 Spoon the mixture into the crab shells or into dishes. Sprinkle with the remaining breadcrumbs and dot with the remaining butter. Bake for 20 minutes. Garnish with the parsley and chives and serve.

PLAICE IN A GREEN JACKET

resh fillets of plaice, wrapped in lettuce, gently poached and served with the lightest white wine sauce.

INGREDIENTS

4 fresh plaice fillets, about 175g/6oz each
1 large head of round lettuce
2 shallots, finely chopped
1 bay leaf
300ml/½ pint/1¼ cups dry white wine
275g/10oz/1¼ cups unsalted butter, softened
15ml/1 tbsp snipped fresh chives
salt and ground black pepper
boiled potatoes, to serve (optional)

SERVES 4

1 Preheat the oven to 180°C/350°F/Gas 4. Using a very sharp knife, skin the plaice fillets. Insert the blade of the knife between the skin and the fillet at the tail end, then, holding the skin with one hand, glide the knife along the skin to remove the fillet.

2 Bring a large saucepan of water to the boil. Separate the lettuce leaves and drop them into the water for 1 minute. Remove with a slotted spoon and refresh under cold water. Drain well.

3 Lay out 3–4 leaves and put a plaice fillet on top. Season well and wrap the leaves around the fish. Top with more leaves, if necessary. Put the fish into a large buttered dish and pour in a little water. Cover with buttered paper and cook for 15 minutes.

4 Meanwhile, put the shallots, bay leaf and white wine into a saucepan. Cook over a high heat for 5 minutes until reduced to about 60–75ml/4–5 tbsp.

5 Remove the bay leaf. Whisk in the butter a little at a time until the sauce is smooth and glossy. Strain into a clean pan. Stir in the chives and season well. Do not boil. Lift the wrapped fish out of the dish and serve with the sauce and boiled potatoes, if liked.

SEAFOOD PIE

T here are as many variations of this dish as there are fish in the sea. You can change the fish and shellfish in this recipe according to what is fresh and available.

INGREDIENTS

450g/1lb fish bones, cleaned
6 peppercorns
1 small onion, sliced
1 bay leaf
750ml/1¼ pints/3 cups cold water
900g/2lb smoked haddock
225g/8oz raw prawns
450g/1lb mussels, cleaned
675g/1½lb potatoes
65g/2½oz/5 tbsp butter
25g/1oz/2 tbsp plain flour
350g/12oz leeks, sliced
115g/4oz small button mushrooms, sliced
15ml/1 tbsp chopped fresh tarragon
15ml/1 tbsp chopped fresh parsley
salt and ground black pepper
fresh tarragon, to garnish

SERVES 4

1 Put the fish bones, peppercorns, onion and bay leaf into a small saucepan with the cold water. Bring to the boil, reduce the heat and simmer for 20 minutes. Remove from the heat and set aside.

2 Meanwhile, put the smoked haddock into a pan with just enough water to cover it. Cover with a piece of buttered paper and simmer for 15 minutes. Drain and cool, then remove the bones and skin and put the flaked fish into a bowl.

3 Drop the prawns into a pan of boiling water and cook until they begin to float. Drain and refresh under cold running water. Peel and discard the shells and add the prawns to the bowl of flaked fish.

4 Place the mussels in a saucepan with 30ml/2 tbsp water. Cover and cook over a high heat for 5–6 minutes until the mussels have opened. Discard any that have not. Refresh under cold water and remove the shells. Put the cooked mussels into the bowl with the fish and prawns.

5 Boil the potatoes for 20 minutes. Drain and dry over a high heat for 1 minute until all traces of moisture have evaporated. Mash with 25g/1oz/2 tbsp of the butter.

6 Meanwhile, melt 25g/1oz/2 tbsp of the butter in a saucepan. Stir in the flour and cook for 1 minute. Strain the fish stock and measure 600ml/1 pint/2½ cups. Whisk a little at a time into the roux until smooth. Cook over a gentle heat for 10 minutes.

7 Preheat the oven to 180°C/350°F/Gas 4. Melt the remaining butter in another saucepan, add the leeks and mushrooms and cook for 4–5 minutes, taking care not to brown them. Add to the fish. Stir in the chopped herbs. Pour in the sauce and fold together, then spoon into a pie dish. Spoon over the mashed potatoes and smooth level with a fork. Place in the oven and cook for 30 minutes. Garnish with the tarragon.

COD WITH PARSLEY SAUCE

Many moons ago, when cod was more plentiful and cheaper than it is today, this was a commonplace, yet undervalued, dish. Perhaps it is time to rediscover just what a delicious recipe it is.

INGREDIENTS

4 cod fillets or steaks, about 225g/8oz each
1 bay leaf
6 peppercorns
small bunch of parsley
1 shallot, quartered
25g/1oz/2 tbsp butter
25g/1oz/2 tbsp plain flour
300ml/½ pint/1¼ cups semi-skimmed milk
salt and ground black pepper
cabbage, to serve (optional)

SERVES 4

1 Grease a large flameproof casserole with a little butter. Lay the four cod fillets in the pan, skin side down. Add the bay leaf, peppercorns, parsley stalks and the shallot.

2 Pour over enough cold water to cover the fish. Slowly bring to the boil and reduce quickly to a gentle simmer. Cook for 5 minutes. Meanwhile, finely chop the parsley tops and set aside.

3 Melt the butter in a saucepan, then stir in the flour and cook gently for 1 minute. Strain the stock from the fish and reserve 150ml/¼ pint/⅔ cup. Remove the fish from the pan and keep warm. Gradually add the reserved stock to the flour mixture and continue stirring over a medium heat until smooth and thickened.

4 Gradually add the milk and bring to the boil. Reduce the heat and cook for about 10 minutes, stirring occasionally. Stir in the chopped parsley and season well. Serve the sauce with the fish and cabbage, if liked.

SALMON WITH SORREL

A luxurious, yet surprisingly light, combination of delicate flavours makes this the perfect recipe for entertaining Irish style.

INGREDIENTS
225g/8oz fish bones
1 small onion, sliced
3–4 peppercorns
1 bay leaf
few parsley stalks
300ml/½ pint/1¼ cups cold water
25g/1oz/2 tbsp butter, melted
4 salmon fillets, about 175g/6oz each
120ml/4fl oz/½ cup dry white wine
300ml/½ pint/1¼ cups single cream
75g/3oz sorrel, washed
salt and ground black pepper

SERVES 4

1 Preheat the oven to 200°C/400°F/Gas 6. Wash the fish bones and put into a saucepan with the onion, peppercorns, bay leaf and parsley stalks. Add the cold water. Bring to the boil, reduce the heat and simmer for 20 minutes.

2 Brush an ovenproof dish with some of the melted butter. Lay the salmon fillets on top and brush with the remaining butter. Bake for 10 minutes, until just cooked.

3 Meanwhile, strain 150ml/¼ pint/⅔ cup of the stock into a saucepan. Add the white wine and cook over a high heat until the liquid is reduced by half.

COOK'S TIP
Sorrel is a herb which grows wild in the countryside and has a refreshing, slightly sour taste reminiscent of lemons. Most readily available in the summer, it is often used in soups and sauces. Make the most of its flavour by adding it at the end of the recipe.

4 Pour in the cream and bring to the boil. Reduce the heat and simmer until the sauce just coats a spoon, then season. Tear the sorrel into pieces and add to the sauce. Cook for 1 minute. Serve with the salmon.

WRAPPED SALMON AND RICE

A close cousin of the Russian Koulibiac, this Irish dish is made with chunks of fresh salmon, combined with mushrooms, eggs and rice in light and flaky pastry.

INGREDIENTS
450g/1lb skinned and boned
fresh salmon fillet
115g/4oz button mushrooms
6 spring onions
50g/2oz/4 tbsp butter
2 eggs, hard-boiled
175g/6oz/1 cup long grain rice, cooked
juice of ½ lemon
450g/1lb puff pastry
1 egg, beaten
salt and ground black pepper
hollandaise sauce, to serve

SERVES 4

1 Preheat the oven to 200°C/400°F/Gas 6. Put the salmon into a saucepan with just enough water to cover it. Poach it gently for 10 minutes until just cooked. Drain and then leave to cool.

2 Roughly chop the mushrooms and finely slice the spring onions. Melt the butter in a saucepan and cook the mushrooms and spring onions for 2–3 minutes. Place them in a mixing bowl.

3 Flake the fish and add to the mushroom and onion mixture. Chop the eggs and stir into the salmon mixture with the rice. Stir in the lemon juice and season well with salt and pepper.

4 Roll out the puff pastry to a rectangle 30 x 35cm/12 x 14in. Brush the edges with egg. Spoon the filling into the centre of the pastry. Join the edges and seal the sides and ends with egg.

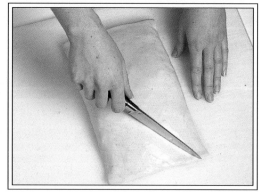

5 Score the top of the pastry with a knife and brush with the remaining egg. Bake for about 30 minutes until golden. Serve hot with hollandaise sauce, or leave to cool completely and serve cold.

COLCANNON

A famous and delicious southern Irish dish which is traditionally served with grilled sausages and bacon.

INGREDIENTS
900g/2lb potatoes
1 Savoy cabbage
50g/2oz/4 tbsp butter
1 small onion, finely chopped
15ml/1 tbsp chopped fresh parsley
salt and ground black pepper

SERVES 4

1 Cut the potatoes into equal chunks. Place in a saucepan and cover with cold water. Bring to the boil, reduce the heat, cover and simmer for 20 minutes.

2 Drain the potatoes and dry out over a high heat for 1 minute until all traces of moisture have evaporated, then mash them.

3 Meanwhile, bring another pan of water to the boil. Break off the outer cabbage leaves and discard. Tear the remaining leaves into pieces and cook in the boiling water for 15 minutes, until just tender.

4 Melt the butter in a large frying pan and heat until hot. Add the chopped onion and cook for 3–4 minutes until just soft.

5 Add the mashed potato and cabbage and fry for 5 minutes, stirring occasionally until it begins to brown around the edges. Stir in the chopped parsley and season well. Serve with grilled sausages and bacon.

GRIDDLE CAKES

These are sometimes called potato cakes or scones, but whatever you call them they are delicious served hot with butter and jam, or with grilled bacon for a hearty breakfast.

INGREDIENTS
225g/8oz potatoes
115g/4oz/1 cup plain flour
1.5ml/¼ tsp salt
1.5ml/¼ tsp baking powder
15g/½oz/1 tbsp butter
25ml/1½ tbsp milk

MAKES 6

1 Cut the potatoes into equal chunks. Place in a saucepan and cover with cold water. Bring to the boil, reduce the heat and simmer for 20 minutes until tender.

2 Drain the potatoes and dry out over a high heat for 1 minute, until all traces of moisture have evaporated. Mash well, making sure there are no lumps left.

3 Sift the flour, salt and baking powder into a mixing bowl. Rub in the butter with your fingertips.

4 Add the mashed potato and mix thoroughly with a fork. Make a well in the centre and pour in the milk. Bring the mixture together to form a smooth dough.

5 Turn out onto a floured board and knead. Roll out to a round 5mm/¼in thick. Cut in half, then cut each half into three triangles.

6 Grease a griddle or frying pan with some butter and heat until very hot. Fry the cakes for 3–4 minutes until golden brown, turning once, then serve hot.

POTATO AND SWEDE STUFFING

An unusual and delicious alternative to the traditional bread and sausagemeat stuffings. This amount is enough to fill a 2.75kg/6lb turkey.

INGREDIENTS

900g/2lb potatoes
1 large swede
115g/4oz/8 tbsp butter
4 streaky bacon rashers, finely chopped
1 large onion, finely chopped
1 large thyme sprig
salt and ground black pepper

SERVES 8

1 Cut the potatoes into equal-size pieces. Place in a saucepan and cover with cold water. Bring to the boil, reduce the heat and cover. Cook for 20 minutes.

2 Meanwhile, cut the swede into chunks. Place in a saucepan and cover with cold water. Bring to the boil, reduce the heat and cook for 20 minutes.

3 Drain both the potatoes and swede and dry out over a high heat for 1 minute, until all traces of moisture have evaporated. Transfer them both to a bowl.

4 Melt the butter in a pan and fry the bacon for 3–4 minutes. Add the chopped onion and fry for a further 3–4 minutes until soft. Sprinkle over the thyme leaves.

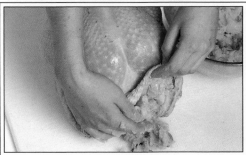

5 Stir into the vegetables. Season well and mash until smooth. Use to stuff turkey and roasts as usual, or put into an ovenproof dish and cover with foil. Bake in the oven for the final hour of the meat's cooking time.

CHAMP

Simple but undeniably tasty, Champ makes an excellent companion for a hearty stew. Use a floury potato such as King Edward.

INGREDIENTS
900g/2lb potatoes
1 small bunch spring onions
150ml/¼ pint/⅔ cup milk
50g/2oz/4 tbsp butter
salt and ground black pepper

SERVES 4

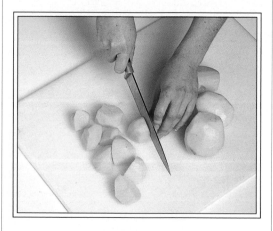

1 Cut the potatoes into even-size chunks, place in a pan and cover with cold water. Bring to the boil, reduce the heat, cover and simmer for 20 minutes until tender.

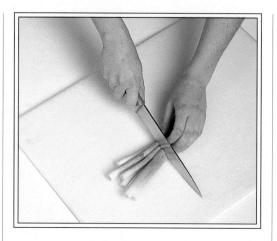

2 Cut the green stems from the spring onions and set aside. Finely chop the remaining onions and put them into a saucepan with the milk. Bring to the boil and simmer until just soft.

3 Drain the potatoes well and put them back into the saucepan. Return to the heat for 1 minute until all traces of moisture have evaporated.

4 Mash the potatoes with the milk and onions and season well. Serve with the butter melting on top and garnish with the chopped green stems of the spring onions.

CHOCOLATE CARRAGHEEN WITH IRISH COFFEE SAUCE

An impressive-looking dessert that is exrememly simple to make. The secret ingredient is sure to keep dinner-party guests guessing.

INGREDIENTS
600ml/1 pint/2½ cups full-cream milk
20g/¾oz carragheen moss
250g/9oz/1¼ cups sugar
115g/4oz plain chocolate
2.5ml/½ tsp groundnut oil
90ml/3fl oz/⅓ cup water
250ml/8fl oz/1 cup strong coffee
15ml/1 tbsp Irish whiskey
grated chocolate, to decorate
lightly whipped cream, to serve

SERVES 4

1 Pour the milk into a heavy-based saucepan. Add the carragheen moss and 25g/1oz/2 tbsp of sugar. Bring to the boil. Reduce the heat and simmer for 15 minutes.

2 Meanwhile, using a sharp chopping knife, chop the chocolate into small pieces or grate roughly. Remove the milk from the heat and stir in the chocolate until it has all melted.

3 Strain the chocolate mixture through a fine strainer. Very lightly grease four teacups with groundnut oil, then pour in the chocolate carragheen. Chill until set.

4 Pour the water and remaining sugar into a heavy-based saucepan. Heat gently, stirring until the sugar dissolves. Remove the spoon and continue to heat the syrup until it turns a pale golden colour.

5 Pour in the coffee and stir over a gentle heat until smooth. Remove from the heat and cool. Stir in the whiskey. Leave to cool.

6 Turn each mousse onto a plate and pour some sauce around each one. Serve with cream and decorate with grated chocolate.

COOK'S TIP
Carragheen moss is a seaweed harvested on the west coast of Ireland. It can be eaten as a vegetable like spinach, but it is also available dried and used as a thickening agent. Look for it in health food shops.

MARMALADE PUDDING

A delicious steamed orange and ginger pudding that is very simple to make. It's tastiest if you use a good quality, tangy, thick-cut peel marmalade that's not too sweet.

INGREDIENTS

115g/4oz/1 cup self-raising flour
pinch of salt
5ml/1 tsp ground ginger
115g/4oz/1 cup shredded suet
115g/4oz/2 cups fresh white breadcrumbs
75g/3oz/8 tbsp dark brown sugar
175g/6oz/8 tbsp marmalade, plus
60ml/4 tbsp to serve
30ml/2 tbsp milk
single cream and orange slices, to serve

SERVES 4–6

1 Grease a 900ml/1½ pint/3¾ cup pudding basin. Sift the flour, salt and ginger into a large bowl. Add the shredded suet, fresh breadcrumbs and sugar and mix thoroughly.

2 Add the marmalade and milk, mixing thoroughly to form a wet, dough-like mixture. Pour into the prepared pudding basin. The mixture should three-quarters fill the bowl. Cover with a double layer of greaseproof paper and secure with string.

3 Steam the pudding for 2½ hours in a double pan with a tight-fitting lid. Check the water halfway through the cooking time.

4 Lift out the basin and remove the paper. Run a knife around the edge of the bowl, invert onto a plate and turn out. Warm the remaining marmalade in a small pan with 30ml/2 tbsp water and serve with the pudding with cream and orange slices.

COOK'S TIP
This pudding is best served immediately as it becomes heavy if left to stand for too long.

PRALIE APPLE PIE WITH HONEY

his deliciously sweet apple pie is made with potato pastry which cooks to a thin crisp crust.

INGREDIENTS
225g/8oz potatoes
115g/4oz/1 cup plain flour
75g/3oz/8 tbsp caster sugar
2.5ml/½ tsp baking powder
pinch of salt
2 cooking apples
1 egg, beaten
30ml/2 tbsp clear honey, to serve

SERVES 4

1 Cut the potatoes into even-size chunks. Put into a saucepan and bring to the boil, then cover and cook for 20 minutes.

2 Drain the potatoes and dry out over a high heat for 1 minute until all traces of moisture have evaporated. Mash well in a bowl. Preheat the oven to 180°C/350°F/Gas 4.

3 Add the flour, 50g/2oz/4 tbsp of the sugar, baking powder and salt and mix thoroughly to form a soft dough.

4 Place the dough on a lightly floured surface and divide it in half. Roll out one half to a 20cm/8in round. Transfer to a lightly greased baking tray.

5 Peel, core and thinly slice the apples. Arrange them on top of the pastry. Sprinkle with the remaining sugar. Brush the edges of the pastry with beaten egg.

6 Roll out the remaining pastry to a 25cm/10in round, then lay it over the apples. Seal the pastry edges together and brush with the remaining beaten egg.

7 Cook in the oven for 30 minutes until golden. Serve hot in slices, with a little honey drizzled over each serving.

CARROT PUDDING

light steamed pudding made with grated carrot, plump sultanas and a hint of orange.

INGREDIENTS
50g/2oz/8 tbsp self-raising flour
5ml/1 tsp baking powder
pinch of grated nutmeg
1 carrot
50g/2oz/1 cup fresh white breadcrumbs
50g/2oz/8 tbsp shredded vegetable suet
50g/2oz/4 tbsp sultanas
grated rind of 1 orange
1 egg
120ml/4fl oz/½ cup semi-skimmed milk
caster sugar and whipped cream, to serve

SERVES 4

1 Lightly grease a 900ml/1½ pint/3¾ cup pudding basin. Sift the flour, baking powder and nutmeg into a mixing bowl.

2 Finely grate the carrot and add to the flour mixture. Stir in the breadcrumbs, shredded suet, sultanas and orange rind.

3 Beat the egg and the milk together, then stir into the dry ingredients to form a smooth dropping consistency.

4 Spoon the mixture into the prepared pudding basin. Cover the basin with two layers of greaseproof paper, folded in the middle to allow room for expansion, and secure with string.

5 Steam for 2 hours in a double pan with a tight-fitting lid. Check the water halfway through the cooking time and top up, if necessary. Remove the greaseproof paper and turn out the pudding on to a plate. Dust with a little caster sugar and serve with chilled whipped cream.

BROWN BREAD ICE CREAM

This uniquely flavoured ice cream could be described as the poor person's praline. Chunks of brown bread are caramelized with brown sugar, then crushed into creamy ice cream.

INGREDIENTS

115g/4oz/2 cups brown breadcrumbs
50g/2oz/4 tbsp soft brown sugar
4 eggs, separated
115g/4oz/8 tbsp caster sugar
150ml/¼ pint/⅔ cup double cream
300ml/½ pint/1¼ cups buttermilk
fresh soft fruit, to serve (optional)

SERVES 4–6

1 Preheat the oven to 200°C/400°F/Gas 6. Put the breadcrumbs onto a baking tray.

2 Sprinkle the brown sugar over the breadcrumbs and place in the oven. Bake for 20 minutes until the sugar has caramelized over the bread. Cool on the tray.

3 Put the egg yolks and caster sugar into a heatproof bowl. Heat a little water in a pan until simmering. Place the bowl with the egg and caster sugar mixture over the pan.

4 Whisk the egg yolks and sugar with an electric whisk for 5 minutes until it looks like mousse and has doubled in bulk. Remove the bowl from the pan and whisk until the mixture holds a trail.

5 Whip the cream until it forms soft peaks. Fold the buttermilk into the cream, then fold into the egg yolk mixture. Break the bread up with a rolling pin and stir into the mixture.

6 Whisk the egg whites until holding soft peaks and fold into the mixture. Pour into a shallow container and freeze for 3 hours.

7 Take out of the freezer and stir with a fork to break up the ice crystals. Freeze until hard. Transfer to the fridge for 30 minutes before serving with fruit.

BREAD PUDDING

Τhis moist fruit pudding is delicious served hot with vanilla ice cream or cold, cut into slices.

INGREDIENTS
450g/1lb/8 thick slices stale white bread
225g/8oz/1¼ cups dried fruit
175g/6oz/¾ cup brown sugar
grated rind of 1 lemon
5ml/1 tsp mixed spice
3 eggs, beaten
15g/½oz/1 tbsp butter
single cream, to serve

SERVES 4–6

1 Preheat the oven to 180°C/350°F/Gas 4. Grease a 20cm/8in round cake tin. Put the bread into a bowl and soak in plenty of water (about 1.2 litres/2 pints/5 cups) for 30 minutes. Drain off the water and squeeze out the excess moisture from the bread.

2 Mash the bread with a fork and stir in the dried fruit, sugar, lemon rind, mixed spice and eggs, until well combined.

3 Spoon the mixture into the prepared cake tin. Dot the top of the pudding with butter, then bake for 1½ hours. Serve warm or leave until completely cool and cut into slices. Serve with single cream. Sprinkled with a little extra brown sugar, if liked.

IRISH COFFEE

T he ultimate Irish beverage, this was invented at Shannon airport to welcome passengers in the cold winter months. It's included in the dessert section because, as the Irish say, "there's eating and drinking in it!"

INGREDIENTS
20ml/4 tsp granulated sugar
600ml/1 pint/2½ cups strong hot coffee
4 measures Irish whiskey
300ml/½ pint/1¼ cups thick
double cream

MAKES 4

1 Divide the granulated sugar among four stemmed, heatproof glasses. Put a metal teaspoon in each glass.

2 Carefully pour in the hot coffee and stir to dissolve the sugar.

3 Stir a measure of whiskey into each glass. Remove the teaspoon and hold it upside-down over the glass.

4 Slowly pour the cream over the back of the spoon on to the hot coffee so that it floats on the surface. Serve at once.

APPLE CAKE

This cake has a thick layer of apples, raisins and hazelnuts baked between sweet sponge. It is just as delicious served cold with sweet whipped cream or yogurt, but you'll be lucky if it lasts that long.

INGREDIENTS

450g/1lb cooking apples
grated rind and juice of 1 lemon
175g/6oz/³⁄₄ cup butter
175g/6oz/1 cup caster sugar
3 eggs, beaten
225g/8oz/2 cups self-raising flour
2.5ml/¹⁄₂ tsp baking powder
2.5ml/¹⁄₂ tsp ground cinnamon
50g/2oz/5 tbsp raisins
30ml/2 tbsp chopped hazelnuts
25g/1oz/4 tbsp icing sugar, to decorate

MAKES A 23CM/9IN CAKE

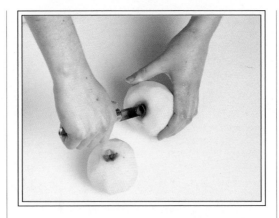

1 Preheat the oven to 180°C/350°F/Gas 4. Grease and base line a 23cm/9in round cake tin. Peel, core and thinly slice the cooking apples. Sprinkle with the lemon juice and set aside.

2 Cream the butter, lemon rind and all but 15ml/1 tbsp of the sugar until light and fluffy. Beat in the eggs a little at a time. Sift the flour and baking powder together. Fold into the creamed mixture.

3 Spoon half of the mixture into the prepared cake tin. Arrange the apple slices on top. Mix the remaining 15ml/1 tbsp of the sugar and the cinnamon together. Sprinkle evenly over the apples.

4 Scatter the raisins and hazelnuts on top. Smooth the remaining cake mixture over the raisins and hazelnuts. Bake for 1 hour. Cool in the tin for 15 minutes, then turn out and dust with icing sugar.

CHOCOLATE POTATO CAKE

This is a very rich, moist chocolate cake, topped with a thin layer of chocolate icing. Use a good quality plain chocolate for best results and serve with whipped cream.

INGREDIENTS
225g/8oz/1 cup caster sugar
240g/8½oz/generous 1 cup butter
4 eggs, separated
275g/10oz plain chocolate
75g/3oz/¾ cup ground almonds
150g/5oz/1¾ cups mashed potato
225g/8oz/2 cups self-raising flour
5ml/1 tsp ground cinnamon
45ml/3 tbsp milk
whipped cream, to serve

MAKES A 23CM/9IN CAKE

1 Preheat the oven to 180°C/350°F/Gas 4. Grease and base line a 23cm/9in round cake tin with greaseproof paper.

2 Cream the sugar and 225g/8oz/1 cup of the butter together until light and fluffy. Beat in the egg yolks one at a time.

3 Chop or grate 175g/6oz of the chocolate and stir into the cake mixture with the ground almonds. Push the mashed potato through a sieve and stir it into the creamed chocolate mixture.

4 Sift the flour and cinnamon together and fold into the mixture with the milk.

5 Whisk the egg whites until stiff, but not dry, and fold into the mixture. Spoon into the lined tin and bake for 1¼ hours. After 45 minutes, cover with greaseproof paper.

6 Allow the cake to cool slightly in the tin, then turn out and cool on a wire rack. Meanwhile, break up the remaining chocolate into a bowl and stand it over a saucepan of hot water. Add the remaining butter in small pieces and stir well until smooth and glossy.

7 Trim the top of the cake so that it is level and smooth over the chocolate icing. Leave to set. Serve with whipped cream.

PORTER CAKE

Porter was a flat, heavy stout named after London's Billingsgate market porters who drank it. It later became very popular in Ireland, but was eventually replaced by the familiar black stouts we know today.

INGREDIENTS
225g/8oz/1 cup butter
225g/8oz/1 cup soft brown sugar
300ml/½ pint/1¼ cups Guinness or
Murphy's stout
675g/1½lb/3 cups mixed
dried fruit
115g/4oz/6 tbsp chopped mixed
candied peel
500g/1¼lb/4 cups plain flour
5ml/1 tsp bicarbonate of soda
5ml/1 tsp grated nutmeg
5ml/1 tsp mixed spice
3 eggs
caster sugar, to decorate

MAKES A 25CM/10IN FRUIT CAKE

1 Grease and base line a 25cm/10in round cake tin with greaseproof paper.

2 Put the butter, sugar and stout into a saucepan and bring slowly to the boil, stirring continuously until all the sugar and butter has melted.

3 Stir in the fruit and peel and bring the mixture to the boil. Reduce the heat and simmer for 5 minutes. Set aside to cool.

4 Preheat the oven to 160°C/325°F/Gas 3. Sift the flour, bicarbonate of soda and spices into a large bowl. Stir in the cold fruit mixture and the eggs until all the ingredients are combined.

5 Spoon into the tin and make a small well in the centre. Bake for 2 hours. Leave to cool in the tin, then sprinkle with caster sugar.

BARM BRACK

This is traditionally a Hallowe'en cake. Long ago, a wedding ring would be baked in it and, it was said, whoever found it would be married within the year.

INGREDIENTS
675g/1½lb/6 cups plain flour
2.5ml/½ tsp mixed spice
5ml/1 tsp salt
7g/¼oz easy-blend dried yeast
50g/2oz/4 tbsp caster sugar
300ml/½ pint/1¼ cups warm milk
150ml/¼ pint/⅔ cup warm water
50g/2oz/4 tbsp butter, softened
50g/2oz/4 tbsp currants
225g/8oz/1 cup sultanas
50g/2oz/5 tbsp chopped peel
milk or syrup, to glaze
icing sugar, to decorate

MAKES A 23CM/9IN CAKE

1 Grease a 23cm/9in round cake tin. Sift the flour, mixed spice and salt together. Stir in the yeast and sugar. Make a well, then pour in the milk and water and mix to a dough. Transfer to a floured board and knead until smooth and no longer sticky. Place in a clean bowl, cover with clear film and leave in a warm place for 1 hour until well risen and doubled in size.

2 Preheat the oven to 200°C/400°F/Gas 6. Add the butter, currants, sultanas and chopped peel and work into the dough. Return to the bowl and cover. Leave to rise for another 30 minutes.

3 Fit the dough into the tin and leave to rise to the top. Brush with milk or syrup and bake for 15 minutes. Cover with foil. Reduce the heat to 180°C/350°F/Gas 4 and bake for 45 minutes. Dust with icing sugar.

CHEESECAKES

T hese little cheesecakes are close cousins of the English Bakewell Tart. Shortcrust pastry is filled with raspberry jam and sponge and topped with a lemon icing and coconut.

INGREDIENTS
115g/4oz/8 tbsp butter
115g/4oz/1 cup caster sugar
rind and juice of ½ lemon
2 eggs, beaten
50g/2oz/8 tbsp self-raising flour
50g/2oz/8 tbsp ground almonds
225g/8oz shortcrust pastry
115g/4oz/8 tbsp raspberry jam
115g/4oz/1 cup icing sugar
25g/1oz/5 tbsp desiccated coconut

MAKES 12

1 Preheat the oven to 190°C/375°F/Gas 5. Beat the butter, caster sugar and lemon rind together until light and fluffy. Beat in the eggs a little at a time.

2 Sift the flour and almonds together and fold into the creamed mixture.

3 Roll out the pastry on a lightly floured surface. Stamp out rounds large enough to fit a 12-cake patty tin. Spoon a little jam into the centre of each.

4 Three-quarters fill each pastry case with the creamed mixture. Bake for 25 minutes until golden brown.

5 Put the icing sugar into a bowl with the lemon juice and enough water to make a thick paste. Spread the glaze lightly over each cake and sprinkle with the coconut. Leave to set.

FRUIT SCONES

T he recipe for scones was brought to Ireland when the English gentry first settled there in the 1800s. The Irish quickly adapted this popular teatime cake to suit their tastes.

INGREDIENTS

225g/8oz/2 cups plain flour
40g/1½oz/3 tbsp butter
15ml/1 tbsp caster sugar
5ml/1 tsp baking powder
50g/2oz/4 tbsp sultanas
2 eggs
25ml/1½ tbsp milk
jam and cream, to serve

MAKES 8

2 Stir in the sugar, baking powder and sultanas and mix well together.

1 Preheat the oven to 200°C/400°F/Gas 6. Sift the flour into a bowl. Rub in the butter with your fingertips.

3 Beat 1 egg. Make a well in the centre of the flour mixture, then mix in the beaten egg and enough milk to form a soft dough.

4 Turn out the dough on to a floured board and knead lightly. Flatten to about 2.5cm/1in thick. Stamp out rounds using a plain cutter. Transfer to a baking tray.

5 Beat the other egg and brush over the scones. Bake for 15–20 minutes. Cool, then serve with jam and cream.

SODA BREAD

Fresh home-made soda bread makes the perfect accompaniment to hearty dishes, such as Leek and Thyme Soup and Coddle.

INGREDIENTS
450g/1lb/4 cups plain flour
5ml/1 tsp salt
5ml/1 tsp bicarbonate of soda
400ml/14fl oz/1⅔ cups buttermilk

MAKES 1 LOAF

1 Preheat the oven to 230°C/450°F/Gas 8. Sift the flour, salt and bicarbonate of soda into a bowl. Make a well in the centre and pour in the buttermilk.

2 Using one hand, slowly incorporate the flour into the milk to give a soft, but not sticky, dough.

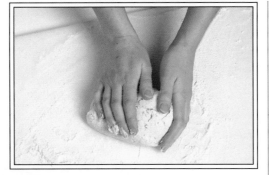

3 Turn on to a floured board and knead lightly for 1 minute until smooth. Smooth and shape to a round about 4cm/1½in high. Cut a deep cross from one edge to the other. Place on a floured baking tray.

4 Bake for 15 minutes. Reduce the heat to 200°C/400°F/Gas 6 and bake for a further 30 minutes. To test if the bread is cooked, tap the underside of the bread which should sound hollow. Cool on a wire rack.

COOK'S TIP
For good soda bread it's important to use buttermilk, as its reaction with the bicarbonate of soda helps the bread rise. If you can't buy buttermilk, use sour milk or sour your own fresh milk with a few teaspoons of lemon juice.

INDEX